VIBE CHECK
BE YOUR BEST YOU

THIS BOOK BELONGS TO:

....

VIBE CHECK
BE YOUR BEST YOU

A CREATIVE JOURNAL

MARGARITA TARTAKOVSKY

STERLING CHILDREN'S BOOKS
New York

STERLING CHILDREN'S BOOKS
New York

STERLING CHILDREN'S BOOKS and the distinctive Sterling Children's Books logo are registered trademarks of Sterling Publishing Co., Inc.

© 2021 Quarto Publishing plc

First Sterling edition published in 2021

ISBN 978-1-4549-4350-1

Distributed in Canada by
Sterling Publishing Co, Inc.
c/o Canadian Manda Group,
664 Annette Street, Toronto,
Ontario M6S 2C8 Canada

For information about custom editions, special sales, and premium and corporate purchases, please contact Sterling Special Sales at 800-805-5489 or specialsales@sterlingpublishing.com.

QUAR.339207

Manufactured in China

Lot #:
2 4 6 8 10 9 7 5 3 1

06/21

sterlingpublishing.com

CONTENTS

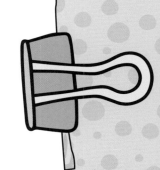

YOUR SAFE, CREATIVE SPACE

BEING A TEEN CAN BE HARD.

MAYBE, AT TIMES, IT FEELS EXCRUCIATING.

ON TOP OF SCHOOL, SOCIAL MEDIA, EXTRA-CURRICULARS, FRIENDS AND FAMILY STUFF, AND A NEVER-ENDING NEWS CYCLE, YOU'RE ALSO UNDERGOING ROLLER-COASTER PHYSICAL CHANGES (HELLO HORMONES!).

AND ON SOME DAYS, IT FEELS LIKE YOUR EMOTIONS WILL SWALLOW YOU WHOLE.

WHILE YOU'VE GOT A LOT GOING ON,
THE GOOD NEWS IS THAT YOU CAN ALSO FEEL BETTER,
EVEN WHEN IT SEEMS LIKE NO ONE LIKES YOU,
YOU'LL NEVER FEEL GOOD ABOUT YOURSELF,
AND YOUR EMOTIONS ARE TOO BIG OR TOO DARK.

Everyone deals with difficult, painful things.

VIBE CHECK IS YOUR PERMISSION-SLIP AND SAFE
SPACE TO EXPLORE ANYTHING THAT'S GOING ON
INSIDE YOUR HEAD AND HEART—NO MATTER HOW
SILLY OR STRANGE IT MIGHT SOUND OR FEEL.
**THINK OF THIS JOURNAL AS YOUR PERSONAL
MOOD-BOOSTING TOOLKIT AND A REMINDER THAT
YOU'RE NEVER ALONE IN YOUR STRUGGLES.**

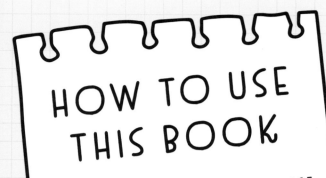

HOW TO USE THIS BOOK

LET'S START WITH SOME GUIDANCE TO HELP YOU UNDERSTAND WHAT TO EXPECT AND HOW TO NAVIGATE THE BOOK.

This journal is interactive, so grab your pencils.

To begin feeling better, use the thought bubbles on pages 10–11 to guide you toward the chapters that can help you with your specific concerns.

Focus on the thoughts or feelings that you relate to.

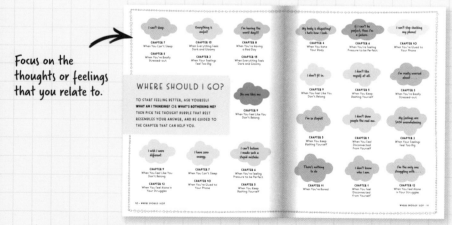

Feel free to skip around, explore, pick out the prompts that call to you, and pass over the ones that don't.

At the start of every chapter, you'll find quick check-ins for seeing where you're at. Before responding, pause and take a deep breath to help you zero in on what's going on.

Circle or tick the options that feel most accurate, or write in your own response.

At the end of the journal, you'll find a list of additional resources for feeling better.

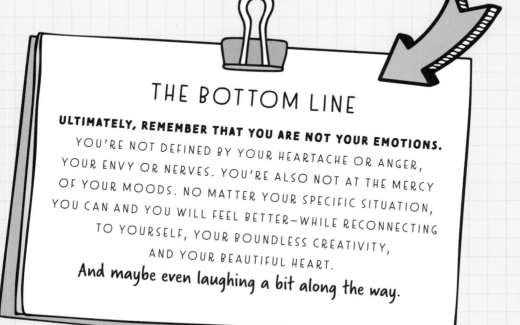

THE BOTTOM LINE

ULTIMATELY, REMEMBER THAT YOU ARE NOT YOUR EMOTIONS. YOU'RE NOT DEFINED BY YOUR HEARTACHE OR ANGER, YOUR ENVY OR NERVES. YOU'RE ALSO NOT AT THE MERCY OF YOUR MOODS. NO MATTER YOUR SPECIFIC SITUATION, YOU CAN AND YOU WILL FEEL BETTER—WHILE RECONNECTING TO YOURSELF, YOUR BOUNDLESS CREATIVITY, AND YOUR BEAUTIFUL HEART. And maybe even laughing a bit along the way.

I can't sleep.

CHAPTER 7
When You Can't Sleep

CHAPTER 5
When You're Really
Stressed-out

Everything is
awful!

CHAPTER 13
When Everything Feels
Dark and Gloomy

CHAPTER 2
When Your Feelings
Feel Too Big

I'm having the
worst day!!!

CHAPTER 8
When You're Having
a Bad Day

CHAPTER 13
When Everything Feels
Dark and Gloomy

WHERE SHOULD I GO?

TO START FEELING BETTER, ASK YOURSELF
WHAT AM I THINKING? OR **WHAT'S BOTHERING ME?**
THEN PICK THE THOUGHT BUBBLE THAT BEST
RESEMBLES YOUR ANSWER, AND BE GUIDED TO
THE CHAPTER THAT CAN HELP YOU.

No one likes me.

CHAPTER 9
When You Feel Like You
Don't Belong

I wish I were
different.

CHAPTER 9
When You Feel Like You
Don't Belong

CHAPTER 12
When You Feel Alone in
Your Struggles

I have zero
energy.

CHAPTER 7
When You Can't Sleep

CHAPTER 10
When You're Glued to
Your Phone

I can't believe
I made such a
stupid mistake.

CHAPTER 6
When You're Feeling
Pressure to be Perfect

CHAPTER 3
When You Keep
Bashing Yourself

My body is disgusting! I hate how I look.

CHAPTER 4
When You Hate
Your Body

If I can't be perfect, then I'm a failure.

CHAPTER 6
When You're Feeling
Pressure to be Perfect

I can't stop checking my phone!

CHAPTER 10
When You're Glued to
Your Phone

I don't fit in.

CHAPTER 9
When You Feel Like You
Don't Belong

I don't like myself at all.

CHAPTER 3
When You Keep
Bashing Yourself

I'm really worried about . . .

CHAPTER 5
When You're Really
Stressed-out

I'm so stupid!

CHAPTER 3
When You Keep
Bashing Yourself

I don't show people the real me.

CHAPTER 1
When You Feel
Disconnected
from Yourself

My feelings are SOOO overwhelming.

CHAPTER 2
When Your Feelings
Feel Too Big

There's nothing to do

CHAPTER 11
When You're Bored

I don't know who I am.

CHAPTER 1
When You Feel
Disconnected
from Yourself

I'm the only one struggling with . . .

CHAPTER 12
When You Feel Alone
in Your Struggles

IT'S EASY TO FEEL DISCONNECTED FROM YOURSELF WHEN THERE'S SO MUCH TO FOCUS ON—SCHOOL, WORK, FRIENDS, FAMILY, FACEBOOK. OR MAYBE YOU FEEL DISCONNECTED BECAUSE YOU HAVEN'T REALLY EXPLORED WHO YOU ARE. THE RESULT?

YOU MIGHT SAY YES TO THINGS YOU DON'T ACTUALLY WANT TO DO.

OR, PERHAPS YOU DO KNOW EXACTLY WHO YOU ARE, BUT YOU'VE KEPT THOSE PARTS HIDDEN. BUT HERE'S THE THING: YOU CAN START EXPLORING OR RECONNECTING TO YOURSELF IN ANY MOMENT—AND START **FILLING YOUR DAYS WITH YOUR LIKES AND LOVES** AND ANYTHING ELSE THAT HONORS YOUR PERSONALITY AND NATURAL PREFERENCES.

YOU CAN TAKE TINY, SAFE STEPS TO REVEAL WHO YOU TRULY ARE.

CHAPTER 1
WHEN YOU FEEL
DISCONNECTED
FROM
YOURSELF

How disconnected do I feel from myself?

1 BEING A BIT DISCONNECTED; 5 BEING "I BARELY KNOW WHO I AM."

Am I proud of who I am?

☐ YES

☐ NO

☐ DEPENDS ON THE DAY OR WHAT I'VE DONE

How often do I show the real me to others?

☐ ALMOST ALWAYS

☐ SOMETIMES

☐ RARELY

☐ ONLY TO CERTAIN PEOPLE

☐ ONLY IN CERTAIN PLACES

MY *Favorites*

JOT DOWN (OR DRAW!) YOUR FAVORITE:

Color	Breakfast	Lunch

Dinner	Dessert

Movie	Book	Song

App

School subject

Word

Joke

Emoji

Game to play

Way to cheer someone up

Way to cheer myself up

Way to spend the weekend

Way to relax

YOUR GOALS, DREAMS, AND WISHES

GRAB MAGAZINES, PHOTOS, ADS, AND ANY OTHER
PAPER MATERIALS. CUT OUT WORDS, QUOTES, AND
IMAGES THAT SPEAK TO WHAT YOU'D LIKE TO ACHIEVE
AND HOW YOU'D LIKE YOUR DAYS TO LOOK—WHICH
COULD BE RIGHT NOW OR IN FIVE YEARS TIME!
PASTE THEM HERE, AND CREATE YOUR OWN
INSPIRING COLLAGE.

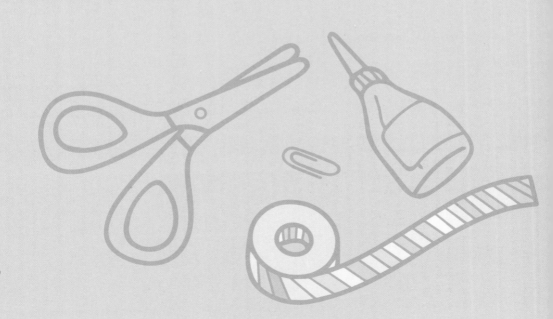

WHEN NO ONE'S WATCHING, I LOVE TO . . .

JOT DOWN ALL THE THINGS YOU LOVE TO DO
WHEN YOU'RE ON YOUR OWN.

....

....

....

....

....

....

....

....

I worry that no one will like the "real" me.

I worry what my friends will think of me.

WHAT STOPS ME FROM BEING ME?

I worry my parents will be upset with me.

I worry the "real" me isn't attractive, interesting, cool, or good enough.

I worry people will make fun of me.

HIDING WHO YOU ARE ONLY HURTS YOU.
WHAT'S ONE TINY ACTION YOU CAN TAKE
TO BE THE TRUE YOU TODAY?

MAYBE ONE OF THESE?

→ PICK UP A KIDS' BOOK YOU'VE BEEN
WANTING TO READ.

→ DELETE FACEBOOK FROM YOUR PHONE
(OR DELETE YOUR ACCOUNT ALTOGETHER).

→ TEXT A FRIEND ABOUT HOW YOU'RE
REALLY FEELING.

→ SIGN UP FOR A MUSIC CLASS.

→ SAY "NO" TO GOING OUT BECAUSE
YOU'D REALLY LIKE TO STAY HOME AND
WATCH A MOVIE WITH YOUR FAMILY.

YOU'RE OVERWHELMED AND FEEL LIKE YOU'RE ABOUT TO EXPLODE. YOU'RE FURIOUS OR HEARTBROKEN—OR BOTH! AND BECAUSE YOUR RED-HOT RAGE AND BONE-DEEP DEVASTATION FEEL SO MASSIVE, YOUR NATURAL IMPULSE MIGHT BE TO PUSH THESE FEELINGS DOWN AND PRETEND THEY DON'T EXIST. OR TO LASH OUT AT A LOVED ONE AND THEN REALLY REGRET IT.

FEELINGS CAN BE CONFUSING SOMETIMES—AND YOU HAVE ZERO CLUE WHAT TO DO WITH THEM. EVEN THOUGH IT SEEMS COUNTERINTUITIVE, THE KEY IS TO **ACCEPT THEM**—AND TO REALIZE THAT WHILE EMOTIONS CAN BE PAINFUL, THEY CAN ALSO BE VALUABLE.

WHEN YOU SLOW DOWN AND LISTEN, YOUR EMOTIONS REVEAL YOUR EXPERIENCES AND NEEDS, SO YOU CAN TAKE HEALTHY ACTIONS. PLUS, THE MORE PRACTICE YOU HAVE WITH FEELING YOUR FEELINGS AND CARING FOR YOURSELF, THE EASIER EXPERIENCING EMOTIONS BECOMES.

CHAPTER 2

WHEN YOUR FEELINGS FEEL TOO BIG

Quick check-in

How strong does this feeling or these feelings feel?

1 BEING LIKE A RAIN SHOWER; 5 BEING A MONSOON.

How overwhelmed do I feel?

1 BEING PRETTY OVERWHELMED; 5 BEING OMG TERRITORY.

Do I feel this way often?

☐ YES

☐ NO

☐ LATELY, IT'S BEEN MORE OFTEN

HOW ARE YOU FEELING?

TO PINPOINT YOUR EMOTION, FIRST SLOOOWWWW
DOWN AND TAKE SEVERAL DEEP BREATHS.

CLOSE YOUR EYES, PUT YOUR HANDS OVER YOUR
HEART, AND SIMPLY ASK YOURSELF:

What's going on
inside right now?

REMEMBER, YOU MIGHT BE
FEELING A FEW DIFFERENT
FEELINGS AT ONCE—WHICH IS
TOTALLY OK. SO, CIRCLE AWAY!

Happy

Energized

Sad

Shocked

Exhausted

Lonely

Anxious

Confident

Confused

Surprised

Embarassed

Heartbroken

Jealous

Panicked

If none of these emotions match yours,
draw your own here.

Hopeless

Let down

Lost

Suspicious

Helpless

Frustrated

Angry

Excited

Disgusted

Disappointed

Relieved

Miserable

Terrified

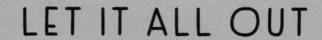

LET IT ALL OUT

PUT ON YOUR FAVORITE MUSIC, AND
DRAW, PAINT, SCRIBBLE, OR COLOR
WHATEVER YOU'RE FEELING RIGHT NOW.

EMOTIONS CAN FEEL LIKE A TIDAL WAVE. SO LET'S RIDE THEM!

FIRST, SCAN YOUR BODY AND NOTICE YOUR PHYSICAL SENSATIONS—WITHOUT JUDGING YOURSELF OR TRYING TO CHANGE HOW YOU FEEL. DRAW YOURSELF ON A SURFBOARD, RIDING YOUR EMOTIONS LIKE YOU'D RIDE THE WAVES—FACING AND EMBRACING THEM AND GOING WITH THE FLOW.

PUT IT ON PAPER

YOUR THOUGHTS CAN HAVE A HUGE IMPACT ON HOW YOU'RE FEELING— AMPLIFYING YOUR ANXIETY, ANGER, AND HURT.

BUT PUTTING THESE OVERWHELMING THOUGHTS ON PAPER CAN HELP TO SHRINK THEM—AND THEREBY LESSEN AND SOFTEN YOUR OVERWHELMING FEELINGS.

WRITE DOWN THE THOUGHTS YOU'RE THINKING.

....

....

....

....

....

....

....

....

THEN, ASK YOURSELF:

> How can I change this thought so it's more helpful and hopeful?

....

....

....

....

....

....

....

KEEP IN MIND: YOU DON'T HAVE TO BELIEVE EVERYTHING YOUR MIND MAKES UP.

HOW CAN I FEEL BETTER?

EVEN THOUGH YOUR EMOTIONS CAN SOMETIMES FEEL PERMANENT, YOU CAN ABSOLUTELY FEEL BETTER—EVEN IF IT'S JUST A BIT BETTER.

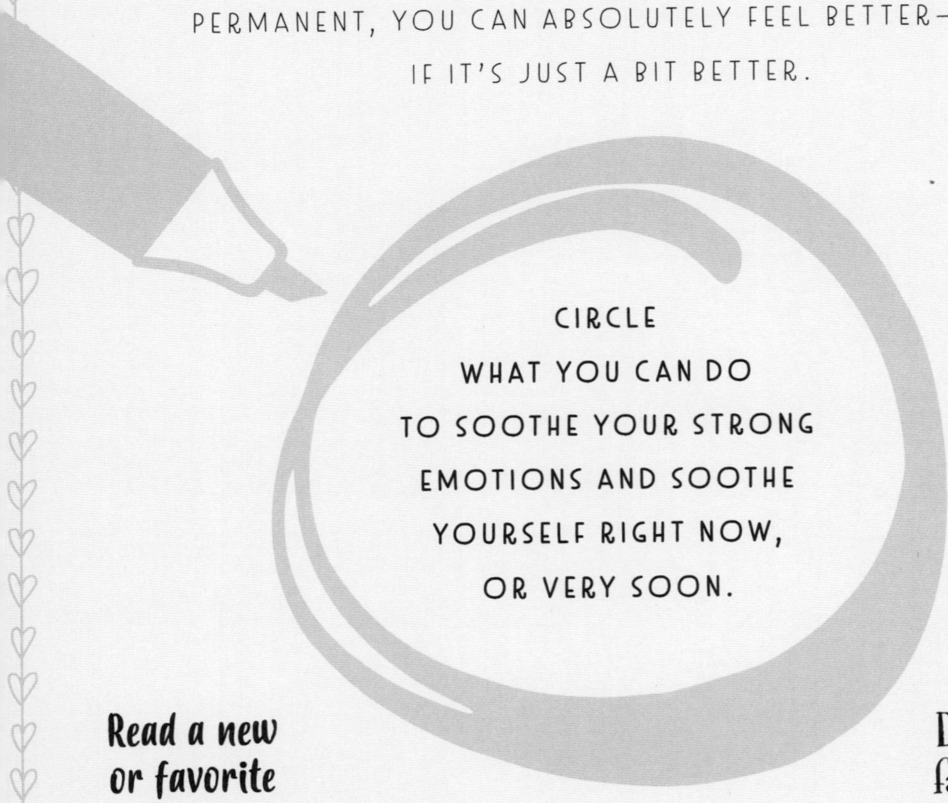

CIRCLE
WHAT YOU CAN DO
TO SOOTHE YOUR STRONG
EMOTIONS AND SOOTHE
YOURSELF RIGHT NOW,
OR VERY SOON.

Read a new or favorite book.

Dance to my favorite song.

Face my fear.

Cry.

Do 50 jumping jacks.

TAKE A WALK.

Hop in the shower (or take a bath).

WATCH A FUNNY MOVIE.

Text my best friend.

Play with my pet or a friend's pet.

Pen a poem.

Stretch my body.

WRITE A SHORT STORY.

Crawl under the covers and take a nap.

Make up a song about my feelings—and sing it!

Take 10 deep breaths or listen to a guided meditation.

Help someone.

Listen to relaxing music.

Do something silly: skip around the house; make funny faces; draw stick figures.

GIVE MYSELF A PEP TALK: "THIS IS REALLY HARD, BUT I'LL GET THROUGH IT."

STEP INTO YOUR
FEELINGS' SHOES . . .

. . . AND WRITE FROM
THEIR PERSPECTIVE.

HERE'S AN EXAMPLE.

My sadness is sad because I got into a fight with a friend. My sadness wants me to fix what happened, or it's telling me that this person isn't the good friend I thought they were. I need to apologize, or stop hanging out with them.

What made my emotion feel this way?

....

....

....

....

What does my emotion want me to know about this situation?

....

....

....

....

What changes does my emotion suggest I make?

....

....

....

....

DON'T KEEP YOUR FEELINGS TO YOURSELF

JOT DOWN THE NAMES OF—OR DRAW—THREE TRUSTWORTHY PEOPLE YOU CAN TURN TO.

1 ....

2 ....

3 ....

Call or text one of them right NOW.

YOU'RE DISGUSTING! AN IDIOT! A LOSER! WHAT'S WRONG WITH YOU? WHY CAN'T YOU DO ANYTHING RIGHT?

YOU'RE OFTEN YOUR OWN WORST CRITIC, PULLING OUT THE MAGNIFYING GLASS AND EXAGGERATING YOUR SUPPOSED FLAWS. AND THE MORE YOUR MIND MAKES THESE MEAN COMMENTS, THE MORE YOU BELIEVE THEM.

BUT THESE AREN'T UNDENIABLE FACTS. THEY'RE OFTEN THE RANDOM CHATTER OF AN INNER CRITIC OR THE HARSH WORDS OF SOMEONE ELSE. EITHER WAY, WHOEVER OWNS THESE WORDS, REMIND YOURSELF THAT THEY'RE FALSE—AND THAT ON THE DAYS YOU FEEL EXTRA SELF-CRITICAL, YOU CAN STILL **TREAT YOURSELF WELL**.

CHAPTER 3
WHEN YOU
KEEP BASHING
YOURSELF

Quick check-in

How bad do I feel about myself?

1 BEING SORTA BAD; 5 BEING "I'M HORRIBLE."

1   2   3   4   5

How often do I have these mean thoughts?

☐ ALL THE TIME

☐ MOST OF THE TIME

☐ SOMETIMES

☐ ONLY WHEN I'M WITH CERTAIN PEOPLE OR DOING CERTAIN THINGS

When do these mean thoughts usually pop up?

☐ AFTER I'VE MADE A MISTAKE

☐ WHEN I FIND OUT SOMEONE IS UPSET WITH ME

☐ WHEN . . .

....

....

....

....

☐ THEY'RE JUST THERE ALL THE TIME

THANKS, INNER CRITIC!

YOU KNOW THOSE CRUEL COMMENTS YOU HEAR INSIDE YOUR
MIND? THAT'S YOUR INNER CRITIC TALKING—WHO ACTUALLY JUST
WANTS TO PROTECT YOU FROM POTENTIAL REJECTION AND HURT.
HOWEVER, YOUR CRITIC IS TOTALLY OVER THE TOP, SO THE NEXT
TIME A MEAN THOUGHT COMES UP, SAY:

Thanks for your concern!
I know you have good intentions,
but I'm all good.
What I really need is kindness.

DRAW YOUR INNER CRITIC ON THE LEFT. ON THE RIGHT, DRAW YOURSELF.
THEN, BELOW, JOT DOWN OTHER THINGS YOU CAN SAY TO YOUR CRITIC
THAT ACKNOWLEDGE THEIR WELL-MEANING MOTIVES AND TELL THEM
YOU'VE GOT IT TAKEN CARE OF.

My inner critic

Me

Now, listen to me inner critic . . .

YES, YOU'RE ALSO AWESOME!

IT'S HARD NOT TO PLAY THE COMPARISON GAME, ESPECIALLY WHEN IT SEEMS LIKE THINGS COME EASIER TO EVERYONE ELSE: YOUR FRIEND LANDS A PART IN THE SCHOOL PLAY AND BARELY PRACTICED; YOUR OTHER FRIEND SCORES AN "A" ON EVERY EXAM WITH MINIMAL STUDYING, WHILE YOU'RE HOLED UP IN YOUR ROOM FOR HOURS AND GET A "C."

INSTEAD, REFOCUS ON YOUR STRENGTHS, BECAUSE YOU'VE CERTAINLY GOT PLENTY.

LIST 10 STRENGTHS NOW—AND COME BACK TO THIS LIST WHENEVER YOU NEED A REMINDER OF HOW INCREDIBLE YOU ARE.

....

....

....

....

....

....

....

....

....

....

....

....

....

....

....

If you're having a tough time, ask a friend or family member to fill up this page with your great qualities, abilities, talents, and skills. Then snap a pic, and reread it any time you need a reminder.

I FORGIVE ME

YOU SCREWED UP. MAYBE EVEN BADLY. BUT HERE'S A FACT:

EVERYONE SLIPS UP!

WRITE YOURSELF A LETTER OF FORGIVENESS.
YOU MIGHT INCLUDE THESE WORDS:

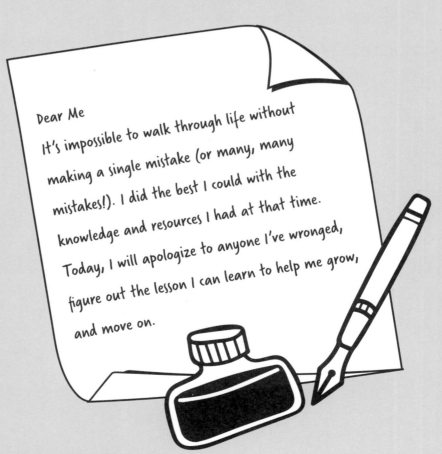

Dear Me

It's impossible to walk through life without making a single mistake (or many, many mistakes!). I did the best I could with the knowledge and resources I had at that time. Today, I will apologize to anyone I've wronged, figure out the lesson I can learn to help me grow, and move on.

THE HERO EMERGES!

SOMETHING HAPPENED AND YOU WERE HUMILIATED. AS
THE PANIC HITS, YOU CRAVE TO DISAPPEAR. YOU PICTURE
YOURSELF BECOMING INVISIBLE, FLYING AWAY, OR
RETREATING INTO SOME MICROSCOPIC HOLE AND NEVER
COMING OUT. SO DON'T—FOR A BIT.

THINK OF YOURSELF AS A COMIC-BOOK HERO WHO'S
BEEN WOUNDED—PHYSICALLY OR EMOTIONALLY,
OR BOTH!—BECAUSE OF A MORTIFYING EVENT.

Draw what happened in the boxes below.
Then, draw your slow but triumphant return.

YOUR OWN
BEST FRIEND

LIST ALL THE WAYS YOU HELP YOUR
BEST FRIEND WHEN THEY FEEL BAD.

．．．

．．．

．．．

．．．

．．．

．．．

．．．

．．．

THEN DO THE
SAME THINGS
FOR YOURSELF!

YOU'RE EXPERIENCING A LOT OF PHYSICAL CHANGES THAT MAKE YOU FEEL WEIRD AND UNCOMFORTABLE IN YOUR OWN SKIN. OR YOU'RE FEELING THE PRESSURE TO LOOK A CERTAIN WAY.

EITHER WAY, YOU DON'T LIKE WHAT YOU SEE IN THE MIRROR. YOU MIGHT EVEN HATE IT. AND YOU THINK IN ORDER TO FEEL BETTER ABOUT YOUR BODY, YOU HAVE TO CHANGE IT. FAST.

BUT YOU DON'T. YOU DON'T HAVE TO CHANGE A THING. OF COURSE, IT'S HARD TO ACCEPT YOURSELF IN A WORLD THAT TELLS YOU THAT YOU MUST LOSE WEIGHT—OR ELSE YOU CAN'T WEAR THAT, GO THERE, OR BE WORTHY OF KINDNESS, APPRECIATION, AND LOVE. BUT HERE'S YOUR PERMISSION TO IGNORE THOSE MESSAGES—REGARDLESS OF WHERE THEY COME FROM—AND TO HAVE FUN, ACT ON YOUR DREAMS, AND ACCEPT YOUR APPEARANCE EXACTLY AS IT IS.

NO EXTERIOR CHANGES NECESSARY.

CHAPTER 4

WHEN YOU HATE YOUR BODY

How much do I hate my body?

1 BEING "I'M NOT A FAN"; 5 BEING "IT'S SERIOUSLY THE WORST!"

How uncomfortable do I feel in my skin?

1 BEING A BIT UNCOMFORTABLE; 5 BEING "I'D LIKE TO CRAWL OUT OF MY SHELL AND TAKE A BREATHER FOR A WHILE."

How often do I feel this uncomfortable?

- ☐ A LOT
- ☐ SOMETIMES
- ☐ JUST RECENTLY
- ☐ ONLY WHEN I'M AROUND CERTAIN PEOPLE
- ☐ ONLY WHEN I'M GOING TO CERTAIN PLACES
- ☐ ONLY WHEN I'M DOING CERTAIN THINGS

I WANT TO . . .

LIST THREE THINGS YOU'RE NOT DOING
(BUT REALLY WANT TO!) BECAUSE OF
HOW YOU FEEL ABOUT YOUR BODY.
ADD ONE TINY STEP YOU CAN TAKE
TO MAKE PROGRESS ON
EACH DEEP DESIRE.

1

I'm not
....
....
I will
....
....

2

I'm not
....
....
I will
....
....

3

I'm not
....
....
I will
....
....

MEDIA CHECK

THE IMAGES AROUND YOU AFFECT HOW YOU
FEEL ABOUT YOUR BODY (AND YOURSELF).
GO TO YOUR INSTA AND OTHER SOCIAL
APPS YOU OFTEN USE AND DOUBLE-CHECK
THE FRIENDS, INFLUENCERS, CELEBRITIES,
AND COMPANIES YOU'RE FOLLOWING.

☐ Does this account make me feel bad about my body?

☐ Does this account tell people what they "should" look like and be like?

☐ Does this account tell people what they should and shouldn't eat?

☐ Do I feel worse after seeing these images?

UNFOLLOW ANYONE YOU ANSWERED "YES" TO.

MY BODY DOES
ALL THIS

DRAW FIVE THINGS YOUR BODY HELPS YOU DO ON A REGULAR
BASIS—FROM DANCING TO WALKING ON THE BEACH TO MAKING ART
TO HUGGING YOUR BEST FRIEND.

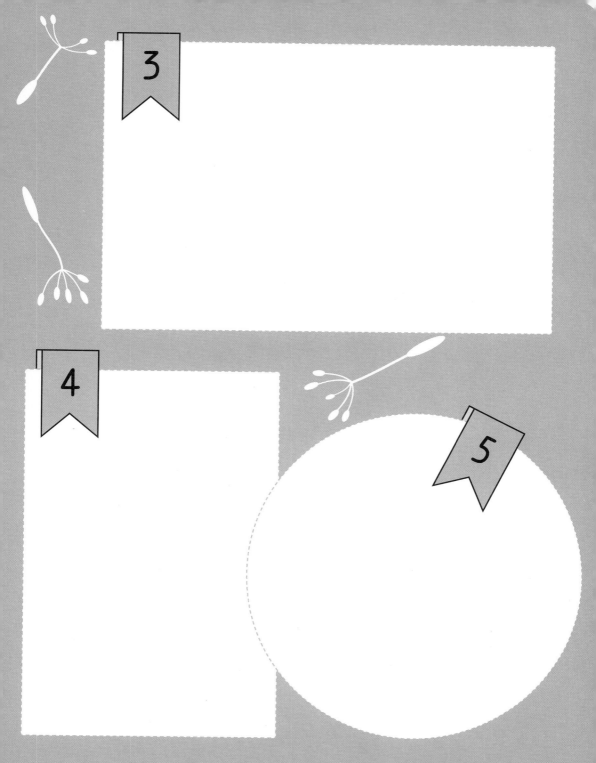

3

4

5

WHERE DOES IT HURT?

SOMETIMES, THE REASON YOU FEEL UNCOMFORTABLE IN YOUR OWN SKIN HAS NOTHING TO DO WITH YOUR PHYSICAL APPEARANCE: RATHER, IT'S BECAUSE YOU'RE ANXIOUS AND TENSE ON THE INSIDE.

DRAW AN OUTLINE OF YOUR BODY AND PUT A HEART NEXT TO WHERE YOU FEEL DISCOMFORT. THEN TOUCH THAT AREA, TAKE SEVERAL DEEP BREATHS, AND SAY TO YOURSELF:

I send comfort, ease, and love here.

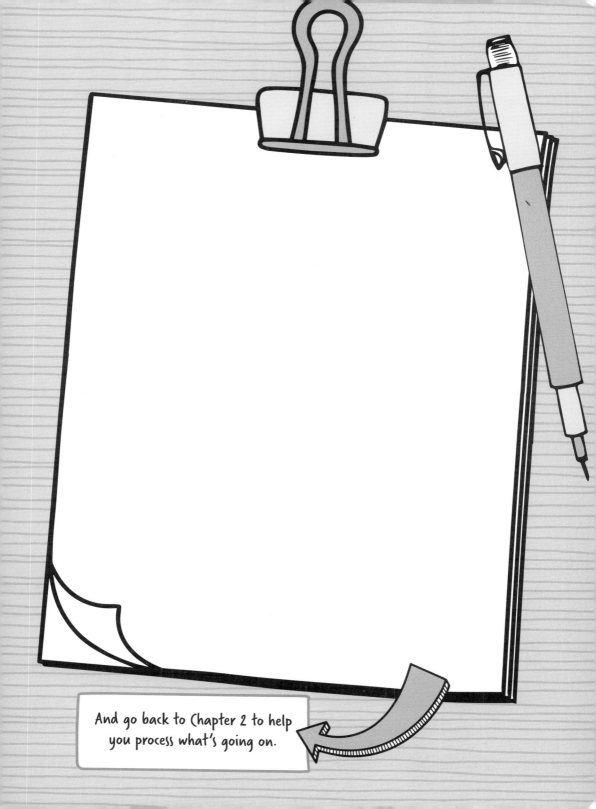

And go back to Chapter 2 to help
you process what's going on.

BIG TESTS. COMPLICATED PROJECTS. LOOMING DEADLINES. SPORTS TRY-OUTS. ENDLESS TO-DO LISTS. FRIENDSHIP OR FAMILY DRAMA. OFTEN, IT FEELS LIKE YOU'RE DEALING WITH A LOT. ON A DAILY BASIS.

BUT EVEN THOUGH YOU'RE FEELING STRESSED-OUT RIGHT NOW, PLEASE KNOW THAT YOU'VE GOT THIS. YOU CAN DEAL WITH WHATEVER COMES YOUR WAY! THE KEY IS TO LEARN HOW TO EFFECTIVELY FACE STRESS.

- FIGURE OUT WHAT'S SPECIFICALLY CAUSING YOU TO FEEL OVERWHELMED.

- CONTROL WHAT ONLY YOU CAN CONTROL.

- REALIZE THAT STRESS ISN'T ALWAYS BAD—IT CAN MAKE YOU WISER AND STRONGER!

CHAPTER 5
WHEN YOU'RE
REALLY
STRESSED-OUT

Quick check-in

How stressed do I really feel?

1 BEING A BIT STRESSED; 5 BEING "YES, OF COURSE, I'M STRESSED-OUT!

WOULDN'T YOU BE?!"

1 2 3 4 5

How often do I feel stressed in a single week?

- [ ] MOST DAYS
- [ ] SOME DAYS
- [ ] A FEW DAYS
- [ ] JUST TODAY HAS BEEN ROUGH

When I'm stressed, what usually happens in my body?

- [ ] MY HEAD FEELS LIKE IT'S GOING TO EXPLODE
- [ ] BUTTERFLIES ARE FLUTTERING INSIDE MY BELLY
- [ ] MY EARS GET HOT
- [ ] I SWEAT
- [ ] I FEEL COLD AND SHAKY
- [ ] MY BODY HURTS
- [ ] ALL OF THE ABOVE

When I'm stressed, what do my thoughts usually sound like?

- [ ] "I CAN'T DO THIS!"
- [ ] "I'LL NEVER GET THIS RIGHT!"
- [ ] "THIS IS TOO MUCH!"
- [ ] SOMETHING ELSE

....

....

....

....

SHRINK

YOUR WORRIES

WHEN WORRIES SWIRL AROUND IN YOUR MIND, THEY FEEL ESPECIALLY OVERWHELMING. WRITING THEM DOWN MAKES THEM FEEL MANAGEABLE.

WRITE DOWN YOUR WORRIES, THEN READ THEM OUT LOUD. SOMETIMES, THIS HELPS YOU TO REALIZE THAT YOUR CONCERNS AREN'T THAT SERIOUS OR STRESSFUL.

Today, I'm worried about . . .

....

....

....

....

Today, I'm worried about . . .

....

....

....

....

Today, I'm worried about . . .

....

....

....

....

TEST YOUR WORRY

PUT YOUR WORRY THROUGH THE STRESS TEST.

JOT DOWN WHAT'S WORRYING YOU.

I'm worried that . . .

....

....

....

....

....

NEXT RESPOND TO THESE QUESTIONS:

WILL THIS MATTER IN:

☐ 1 WEEK   ☐ 1 MONTH   ☐ 1 YEAR   ☐ 5 YEARS?

IF **NO**, GREAT! GO DO SOMETHING *fun!*

IF YES, JOT DOWN WHY THIS WORRY MATTERS.

....

....

....

....

....

NEXT, JOT DOWN ONE SMALL STEP YOU CAN TAKE TO REDUCE
THE WORRY (WHICH ONLY YOU HAVE CONTROL OVER).

For example, you're worried you won't make the basketball team, so you identify what
you need to work on. Then, you text your friend to help you practice those drills.

....

....

....

....

....

OF COURSE, SOMETIMES, NO MATTER WHAT YOU DO, YOU DON'T
GET THE OUTCOME YOU WANTED. AND YOU FEEL EVEN MORE
STRESSED. WHEN THAT HAPPENS, LOOK FOR THE LESSON
(AND SKIP TO PAGE 80 TO ADJUST YOUR ATTITUDE).

TURN STRESSORS
INTO SOLUTIONS

STRESSOR: I'm worried I'm going to fail the test. Again.
SOLUTION: What specific actions can I take right now and this week to improve my test performance?
STEPS: Today, I'll study for two hours, and take a five-minute break after every 30 minutes. I'll talk to my parents about hiring a tutor. Tomorrow, I'll ask my teacher for extra help.

Now it's your turn

STRESSOR: I'm worried that . . . .

....

SOLUTION: What can I do right now and this week to . . . .

....

STEPS: Today, I'll . . . .

....

Tomorrow, I'll . . . .

....

STRESSOR: I'm worried that . . .

....

SOLUTION: What can I do right now and this week to . . .

....

STEPS: Today, I'll . . .

....

            Tomorrow, I'll . . .

....

STRESSOR: I'm worried that . . .

....

SOLUTION: What can I do right now and this week to . . .

....

STEPS: Today, I'll . . .

....

            Tomorrow, I'll . . .

....

MEDITATIVE MANDALAS

COLORING OR DRAWING A MANDALA CAN BE CALMING.

Get coloring and see how you feel.

Now sketch your own and color that in too.

ADJUST YOUR ATTITUDE

STRESS ISN'T ALWAYS AWFUL. IT CAN ACTUALLY BE A GOOD THING! STRESSFUL SITUATIONS PREPARE YOU TO FACE ALL KINDS OF INEVITABLE CHALLENGES IN LIFE.

List times when stressful situations helped you learn and grow.

....

....

....

....

....

....

....

....

....
....
....
....
....
....
....
....
....
....
....
....
....
....
....
....
....
....

OH NO! YOU MADE A MISTAKE. MINOR OR MASSIVE, IT DOESN'T REALLY MATTER, BECAUSE YOU DESPISE SLIP-UPS. BECAUSE IF IT'S NOT FLAWLESS, THEN IT SUCKS (AND SO DO YOU). OR, YOU YEARN TO DO WELL IN SCHOOL, GET THE SCHOLARSHIP, AND ACHIEVE GREAT THINGS—BUT LATELY YOUR GRADES HAVE BEEN SLIPPING OR THE STUDY MATERIAL HAS GOTTEN HARDER. AND YOU CAN'T KEEP UP.

STRIVING FOR PERFECTION IS EXHAUSTING. EVEN MORE SO, PERFECTION DOESN'T EXIST—OR IT CAN'T EXIST FOREVER.

YOU'RE BOUND TO MAKE MISTAKES, MAKE SOMEONE ANGRY, GET A LESS-THAN-STELLAR GRADE, AND TAKE A WRONG TURN IN YOUR LIFE. WHILE IT'S GREAT TO BE CONSCIENTIOUS AND STRIVE TO PRODUCE EXCELLENT WORK, PUTTING TOO MUCH PRESSURE ON YOURSELF ONLY SPARKS ANXIETY AND SAPS YOUR HAPPINESS.

CHAPTER 6

WHEN YOU'RE FEELING
PRESSURE
TO BE
PERFECT

Quick check-in

How much do I fear making mistakes?

1 BEING PRETTY AFRAID; 5 BEING "SO MUCH SO, IT'S PARALYZING."

1   **2**   **3**   **4**   **5**

How often do I strive for perfection?

☐ ALL THE TIME   ☐ MOST OF THE TIME

☐ SOMETIMES   ☐ I JUST STARTED DOING THIS RECENTLY

☐ ONLY WITH SOME THINGS, LIKE . . .

....

....

....

Why do I really strive for perfection?

☐ BECAUSE I WORRY THAT OTHERS WILL DISLIKE OR REJECT ME

☐ BECAUSE MY PARENTS SAY IT'S IMPORTANT

☐ BECAUSE IF IT'S NOT PERFECT, THEN I'M A FAILURE

☐ BECAUSE . . .

....

....

....

....

MAKE A MASSIVE MESS

TO GET MORE COMFORTABLE WITH **ImpeRFecTioN**, AND EVEN SEE THE FUN IN IT, MAKE A HUGE MESS ON THIS PAGE.

Pour coffee, juice, or soda on this page—or some other hot or cold drink.

PASTE RANDOM PAPERS.

Rub in some dirt or sand.

Cover the page using all the crayons and markers in your home.

DRAW SOMETHING REALLY UGLY

USE THIS SPACE TO DRAW THE UGLIEST THING YOU'VE **EVER** SEEN.

imPErfectiON
IS A GREAT TEACHER

REFLECT ON A MISTAKE YOU'VE MADE. CIRCLE ANY
OF THE LESSONS YOU LEARNED AND WRITE A BIT
MORE ABOUT THEM.

I learned a
different way
to study.

I learned
what
not to do.

I learned
to be kinder
to others.

I LEARNED
TO BE MORE
FLEXIBLE.

....

....

....

....

I learned
what I
don't like.

....

I learned
something
important
about myself.

....

....

I LEARNED
NOT TO MAKE
ASSUMPTIONS.

....

I learned
to take
responsibility.

....

....

I learned what
really matters
to me.

....

YOUR ANXIOUS Companion

SOMETIMES, YOU WAIT TO PURSUE YOUR WANTS
AND WISHES UNTIL YOU FEEL ZERO SELF-DOUBT,
UNTIL YOU CAN DO IT PERFECTLY AND GRACEFULLY,
WITHOUT ANY SWEAT UNDER YOUR ARMPITS.

BUT YOUR ANXIETY MAY NOT GO AWAY—WHICH
IS USUALLY PRETTY COMMON FOR
MOST PEOPLE.

PICTURE YOUR ANXIETY AS A PERSON

Draw yourself and your anxiety doing whatever it is you're anxious about doing (but still really want to do). Then do it anyway, as your anxiety walks, sits, runs, leads, and creates alongside you. Maybe your anxiety doesn't have to be your enemy. Maybe it can be a neutral acquaintance, or even become a concerned, kind friend.

AN ImPERfect LIST

LIST ALL THE IMPERFECT THINGS YOU LOVE.

For example, your grandma's wrinkly face, your best friend's crooked smile, glue and glitter all over your hands, and your favorite faded, holey sweatshirt.

IT'S HARD TO FEEL GOOD WHEN YOU'RE NOT GETTING ENOUGH SLEEP. SLEEP NOT ONLY BRIGHTENS YOUR MOOD AND REDUCES ANXIETY; IT ALSO SUPPORTS YOUR DEVELOPING BRAIN AND PHYSICAL HEALTH. PLUS, OVER TIME, NOT GETTING THE RECOMMENDED EIGHT TO 10 HOURS OF SLEEP CAN INCREASE YOUR CHANCES OF GETTING HURT, HAVING DEPRESSION, OR NOT BEING ABLE TO FOCUS.

IF YOUR SCHEDULE IS PACKED, GETTING THAT MUCH **SLEEP MIGHT SEEM IMPOSSIBLE.** BUT YOU CAN GET PRETTY CLOSE BY **ADOPTING SOME PRO-SLEEP HABITS.**

(IF YOU CAN'T SLEEP BECAUSE YOU'RE WORRIED ABOUT SOMETHING, FLIP TO CHAPTER 5 ON STRESS.)

CHAPTER 7

WHEN YOU CAN'T SLEEP

Quick check-in

How's my sleep been in the last week or so?

☐ NOT BAD

☐ NOT GREAT

☐ SLEEP? WHAT'S THAT?

How tired do I feel right now?

1 BEING NOT THAT TIRED; 5 BEING "I COULD SLEEP FOR 10 DAYS STRAIGHT."

How energized have I been on most mornings?

1 BEING POPPING OUT OF BED AND READY TO SEIZE THE DAY;

5 BEING, "I CAN'T REMEMBER MY NAME AND WHAT PLANET I LIVE ON."

ZZZ

BORE YOURSELF TO BED

BOREDOM CAN ACTUALLY BE AN EFFECTIVE
SLEEPING TOOL—JUST THINK ABOUT HOW
HARD IT IS TO KEEP YOUR EYES OPEN WHEN
YOUR TEACHER DRONES ON ABOUT . . .
YOU CAN'T EVEN RECALL.

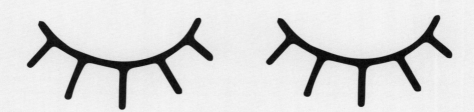

ON THIS PAGE, WRITE ABOUT THE MOST BORING THING YOU RECENTLY LEARNED, HEARD, OR WERE SUPPOSED TO LEARN IN SCHOOL. WRITE ABOUT IT OVER, AND OVER, AND OVER.

....

....

....

....

....

....

....

....

....

....

....

....

....

....

....

....

....

COLORING SHEEP

TO WIND DOWN AND RELAX
YOUR MIND, USE CALMING
COLORS TO COLOR IN
EACH SHEEP.

When you're done,
count them.

SOOTHING SKETCHING

SKETCH A SCENE THAT SOOTHES YOU—SUCH AS
A BEACH, FOREST, FIELD OF FLOWERS,
STAR-FILLED SKY, A PATIO WITH STRING
LIGHTS AND CANDLES, OR FLUORESCENT FISH
SWIMMING IN DEEP BLUE WATERS.

BREATHE BETTER

TAKING DEEP BREATHS RELAXES YOUR NERVOUS
SYSTEM SO YOU'RE CALM ENOUGH TO FALL ASLEEP.

INHALE FOR FOUR SECONDS,
HOLD YOUR BREATH
FOR SEVEN SECONDS,
THEN EXHALE
FOR EIGHT SECONDS.

1234

1234567

12345678

IF THAT FEELS UNCOMFORTABLE,
BREATHE IN FOR A COUNT OF FOUR,
AND BREATHE OUT FOR A COUNT OF FOUR.

AS YOU PRACTICE THIS BREATHING TECHNIQUE,
DOODLE ON THIS PAGE.

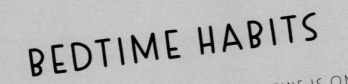

BEDTIME HABITS

CREATING A CALMING BEDTIME ROUTINE IS ONE OF THE BEST WAYS TO FALL ASLEEP FASTER. TRY TO TAKE THE SAME STEPS EVERY NIGHT, ABOUT 30 TO 45 MINUTES BEFORE BED.

- ☐ Keep devices out of my room.
- ☐ Listen to a guided meditation.
- ☐ Read a relaxing book.
- ☐ Jot down one thing I appreciated about today.
- ☐ Take a warm shower or bath.
- ☐ Gently stretch my body.

TICK THE HABITS YOU'LL START DOING—OR WRITE IN YOUR OWN.

My own sleep-promoting ideas are:

zzz...

WOKE UP ON THE WRONG SIDE OF THE BED?
DIDN'T GET MUCH SLEEP? FEELING IRRITATED,
SUPER-SENSITIVE, OR JUST ALL-AROUND BLAH?

ON SOME DAYS, EVEN THOUGH THE SUN IS SHINING
AND LIFE IS GOOD, **YOU'RE IN A BAD MOOD,**
HAVING A BAD DAY. YOU'RE FRUSTRATED,
ANNOYED, AND MAYBE EVEN FURIOUS.

THANKFULLY, YOU CAN **TURN THINGS AROUND AND
FEEL BETTER WITH A FEW SMALL STEPS.**

CHAPTER 8
WHEN YOU'RE HAVING A
BAD DAY

Quick check-in

How blah, bad, annoyed, or tender do I feel?

1 BEING QUITE A BIT; 5 BEING OFF THE CHARTS!

How often do I feel this way?

- ☐ ALL THE TIME
- ☐ JUST TODAY
- ☐ MOST OF THE TIME
- ☐ JUST THIS WEEK
- ☐ SOMETIMES
- ☐ WHEN . . .

....

....

....

USUALLY ON BAD DAYS, THIS IS WHAT I DO, WHICH ONLY MAKES ME FEEL WORSE:

....

....

....

....

DAILY GIFTS AND COMFORTS

A QUICK WAY TO FEEL BETTER IS TO THINK ABOUT THE
PEOPLE, PLACES, AND THINGS THAT YOU'RE GRATEFUL FOR.
SO, FILL THE FIRST JAR WITH EXACTLY THAT.

THIS
I'M
GRATEFUL
FOR

IF YOUR MOOD IS STILL SOUR, THAT'S OK! FILL THE
SECOND JAR WITH COZY, COMFORTING THINGS YOU
CAN SAVOR RIGHT NOW TO FEEL BETTER, SUCH AS
HOT TEA, A HUG, A JUST-OUT-OF-THE-DRYER
BLANKET, OR YOUR FAVORITE BOOK.

THIS
I TAKE
COMFORT
IN

Shake it off— *literally!*

PUT ON A GOOD SONG,
CLOSE YOUR EYES, AND
LITERALLY SHAKE DIFFERENT
PARTS OF YOUR BODY TO
SHAKE OFF YOUR BAD MOOD.
START BY SHAKING YOUR RIGHT HAND,
MOVING TO YOUR RIGHT ARM, THEN YOUR
LEFT HAND, THEN YOUR LEFT ARM. DO THE
SAME WITH YOUR FEET AND LEGS. SET A
TIMER FOR 10 MINUTES (YES, REALLY!),
AND SHAKE YOUR ENTIRE BODY.
SHAKE OFF THE FRUSTRATION,
THE EMPTINESS, OR ALL-AROUND
BAD VIBES.

Draw how you feel or anything that popped up while you were shaking.

EMPOWER
yourself!

WRITE DOWN WHAT MAKES YOU FEEL STRONG, CAPABLE, AND RESILIENT, SUCH AS: RUNNING; LISTENING TO YOUR FAVORITE SONGS; PLAYING SOCCER; REREADING AN INSPIRING QUOTE; OR GETTING AN ENCOURAGING PEP TALK FROM YOUR COUSIN.

....

....

....

....

....

....

....

....

....

....

....

....

....

....

....

NOW DO ONE OF THESE THINGS. **RIGHT NOW!**

HUNT FOR BEAUTY

SKETCH ONE BEAUTIFUL THING YOU'VE SEEN TODAY, OR ONE
BEAUTIFUL THING THAT HAPPENED. MAYBE YOUR BEST FRIEND
TRIED TO CHEER YOU UP; OR, YOUR PARENTS PATIENTLY
LISTENED TO YOUR PAIN.

Maybe you saw a flower blooming from a tiny crack in the street.

DECLUTTER AND DECORATE

DECLUTTERING AND REDECORATING YOUR ROOM CAN HELP YOU FEEL LESS STRESSED AND MORE COMFORTABLE. TO SPRUCE UP YOUR SPACE AND CREATE YOUR OWN CALMING, CREATIVE SANCTUARY, USE THIS CHECKLIST.

- [ ] Draw a new piece of art and frame it.
- [ ] Move your furniture around.
- [ ] Toss or donate 10 items from your room.
- [ ] Donate 10 pieces of clothing.
- [ ] Declutter and clear your desk.
- [ ] Hang some string lights or buy/pick some fresh flowers.
- [ ] Wash your sheets and make your bed.
- [ ] Create a collage with images that inspire you and put it above your desk or bed.

YOU FEEL LIKE AN OUTSIDER. AN OUTCAST. AN ALIEN.
SERIOUSLY, ON SOME DAYS YOU WONDER IF
YOU ARRIVED HERE FROM ANOTHER PLANET.

IT FEELS LIKE NO ONE UNDERSTANDS YOU
OR APPRECIATES YOUR QUIRKS. YOUR SOCIAL
MEDIA POSTS DON'T GET MANY LIKES. MAYBE
A FEW FRIENDS HAVE UNFOLLOWED YOU.
EVEN WITH YOUR CLOSEST PEOPLE, YOU
SOMETIMES FEEL AWKWARD AND ALONE.

BUT YOU KNOW WHAT?

THESE FEELINGS ARE COMPLETELY NORMAL,
ESPECIALLY WHEN YOU'RE GOING THROUGH
SO MANY PHYSICAL AND EMOTIONAL CHANGES.

CHAPTER 9

WHEN YOU FEEL LIKE

YOU DON'T BELONG

Quick check-in

Right now, how intense are my feelings of being an outsider?

1 BEING PRETTY STRONG; 5 BEING "I'M CLEARLY FROM ANOTHER PLANET."

1   2   3   4   5

How often do I feel out of place with my friends?

☐ ALL THE TIME   ☐ MOST OF THE TIME   ☐ SOMETIMES

☐ RARELY   ☐ ONLY WHEN . . .

....

....

WHEN I FEEL LIKE AN OUTSIDER, I'M [FEELING] . . .

....

....

. . . AND I WANT TO [BEHAVIOR].

....

....

THE MORE HELPFUL, HEALTHIER OPTION IS TO [ACTION YOU CAN TAKE] . . .

....

....

....

....

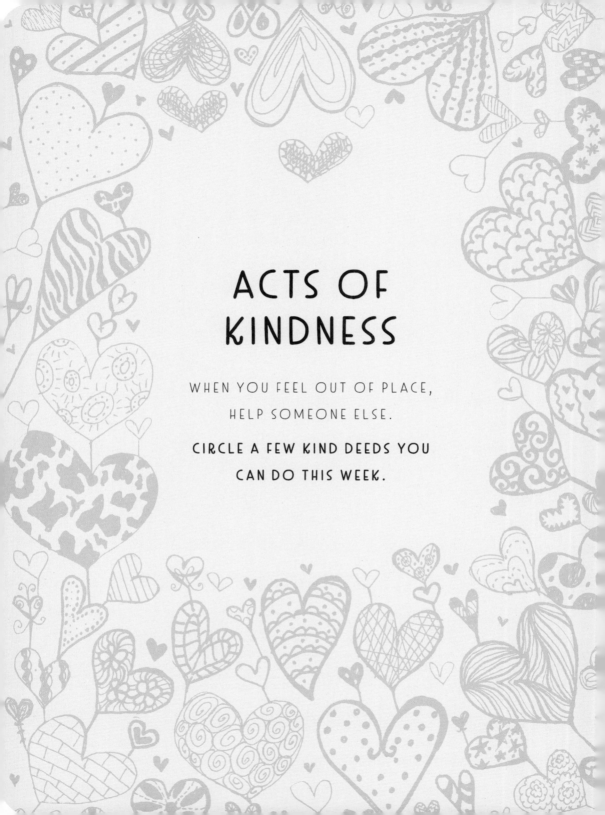

ACTS OF KINDNESS

WHEN YOU FEEL OUT OF PLACE,
HELP SOMEONE ELSE.

CIRCLE A FEW KIND DEEDS YOU
CAN DO THIS WEEK.

Find a creative way to bring a little joy to someone.

FIND A PLACE TO VOLUNTEER YOUR TIME OR SKILLS.

Sit next to someone who usually sits alone.

Leave a few sticky notes with positive messages around your school.

Thank a favorite teacher.

Help a family member with a chore.

Help an elderly neighbor with a tough task.

COMPLIMENT A CLASSMATE.

Write a thank-you note to your favorite aunt (uncle, cousin, grandparent)—and mail it.

I
SEE
ME

GRAB A MIRROR (OR YOUR PHONE'S CAMERA) AND
LOOK INTO YOUR EYES. DRAW THEM IN THE MIRROR
ON THE OPPOSITE PAGE.

THEN WRITE SELF-COMPASSIONATE STATEMENTS
AROUND YOUR SKETCH, LIKE:

I see myself.

I am proud of who I'm becoming.

Maybe I don't fit in with some people at school,
but I still appreciate myself, and I deserve to be happy.

FIND CONNECTIONS

PEOPLE OFTEN CONNECT WITH INDIVIDUALS WHO LIKE SIMILAR THINGS. TO FIND NEW FRIENDS, FIGURE OUT WHAT YOU LIKE TO DO.

IN THIS COLUMN, MAKE A LIST OF YOUR INTERESTS.

IN THIS COLUMN, JOT DOWN THE SCHOOL CLUBS, OUT-OF-SCHOOL ORGANIZATIONS, AND ONLINE GROUPS THAT EXIST FOR EACH INTEREST.

Which one can you join this week?

DON'T FIT IN?
NO PROBLEM!

EVEN THOUGH IT FEELS PAINFUL AT TIMES,

NOT FITTING IN CAN BE A GOOD THING!

REALLY!

BECAUSE IT MEANS YOU'RE BEING TRUE TO YOURSELF AND YOUR UNIQUE TRAITS. YOU'RE NOT PRETENDING OR WEARING A MASK. YOU CAN PARTICIPATE IN ACTIVITIES YOU GENUINELY LIKE VERSUS STAYING IN SOMETHING YOU DON'T (AND FEELING MISERABLE).

NAME A FEW OTHER REASONS WHY IT'S OK, EVEN GOOD, NOT TO FIT IN. IF YOU'RE COMING UP SHORT, ASK AROUND! INTERVIEW OLDER RELATIVES, NEIGHBORS, AND TEACHERS (YEP, THEY WERE YOUNG ONCE), AND INCLUDE THEIR ANSWERS HERE.

FLIP THE SCRIPT!

YOUR MIND INVENTS ALL KINDS OF (OFTEN FALSE) STORIES ABOUT WHY YOU DON'T FIT IN.

JOT DOWN THESE UNTRUE STORIES HERE. THEN REWRITE THEM SO THEY'RE ACTUALLY EMPOWERING, ENCOURAGING, AND SUPPORTIVE.

old, hurtful story

New, kind story

Old, hurtful story

New, kind story

Old, hurtful story

New, kind story

YOUR PHONE IS YOUR CONNECTION TO YOUR FRIENDS, YOUR FAVORITE APPS, YOUR SCHOOL, AND REALLY THE ENTIRE WORLD. SO, IT'S UNDERSTANDABLE THAT YOU LOVE IT AND CAN'T GET ENOUGH.

BUT TOO MUCH SCREEN TIME CAN ALSO SINK YOUR ENERGY AND SHIFT YOUR ATTENTION AWAY FROM OTHER IMPORTANT WAYS THAT YOU CONNECT TO LOVED ONES, YOUR WORLD, AND YOURSELF.

WHETHER YOU REALIZE THAT YOU NEED A BREAK, OR YOUR PARENTS HAVE REALIZED IT FOR YOU, YOU'RE PROBABLY WONDERING, WHAT THE HECK DO I DO WITHOUT MY PHONE?

CHAPTER 10
WHEN YOU'RE
GLUED
TO YOUR
PHONE

Quick check-in

How many hours a week do I use my phone?

- [ ] LESS THAN 7 HOURS
- [ ] 8-12 HOURS
- [ ] 13-17 HOURS
- [ ] 18-22 HOURS
- [ ] OVER 23 HOURS

How do I typically feel when I'm using my phone?

☐ ENERGIZED   ☐ NEUTRAL   ☐ SAD   ☐ ENVIOUS

☐ CALM   ☐ HAPPY   ☐ SOMETHING ELSE

....

....

How do I typically feel after using my phone?

☐ ENERGIZED   ☐ NEUTRAL   ☐ SAD   ☐ ENVIOUS

☐ CALM   ☐ HAPPY   ☐ SOMETHING ELSE

....

....

What tends to make me feel bad when I'm on my phone?

....

....

....

How do I feel when I can't use my phone?

☐ HELPLESS   ☐ RELIEVED   ☐ ANNOYED   ☐ RELAXED

☐ ANGRY   ☐ BORED   ☐ SOMETHING ELSE

....

....

TAKE THIS JOURNAL ON A 10-MINUTE WALK . . .

. . . AND DRAW

WHAT I SEE

WHAT I HEAR

WHAT I SMELL

WHAT I TASTE

WHAT I FEEL

TAKE A
REAL BREAK

PEOPLE OFTEN PULL OUT THEIR PHONES WHEN
THEY NEED A BREAK. BUT SCROLLING AND
REFRESHING AREN'T ACTUALLY RELAXING.

ON THE OPPOSITE PAGE, CREATE SOMETHING THAT FEELS GENUINELY CALMING.

Maybe . . . Draw a pretty space • Draw candles burning • Draw yourself doing yoga • Draw the night sky

DRAW YOUR DREAM APP

What my app is called

....

....

....

What my app does

....

....

....

Why my app is so helpful

....

....

....

What others think about my app

....

....

....

....

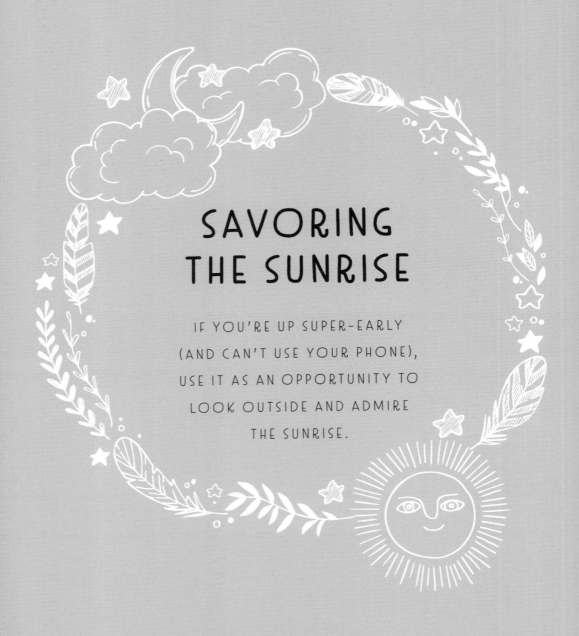

SAVORING THE SUNRISE

IF YOU'RE UP SUPER-EARLY
(AND CAN'T USE YOUR PHONE),
USE IT AS AN OPPORTUNITY TO
LOOK OUTSIDE AND ADMIRE
THE SUNRISE.

SKETCH WHAT YOU SEE.

SEASONAL SOUVENIRS

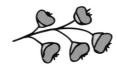

LOOK FOR EVIDENCE OF THE CURRENT SEASON—SUCH AS FALL LEAVES, SEEDS, WILDFLOWERS—AND PASTE YOUR TREASURES HERE.

SCAVENGER HUNT

THIS WEEK, KEEP AN EYE OUT FOR THE BELOW,
AND DRAW EACH ONE WHEN YOU FIND IT.

→ Clouds that look like waves, mountains, castles, or people
→ A bright-colored door
→ A work of art
→ Something blue
→ A sweet scent
→ Something yellow
→ A blooming flower
→ A super-tall tree

BOREDOM CAN FEEL INCREDIBLY UNCOMFORTABLE, WHICH EXPLAINS WHY PEOPLE RUSH TO MAKE IT DISAPPEAR. USUALLY YOU SCRATCH THE ITCH WITH YOUR PHONE OR SOME OTHER LESS-THAN-HEALTHY ACTIVITY.

INSTEAD, AS YOU FEEL THE FIRST PANGS OF BOREDOM, PAUSE AND EASE THE TENSION—TRY STRETCHING YOUR BODY AND TAKING FIVE DEEP BREATHS.

THEN **RETHINK BOREDOM**. VIEW IT AS AN OPPORTUNITY TO **DISCOVER SOMETHING NEW** AND INTERESTING—ABOUT YOUR WORLD AND ABOUT YOURSELF.

CHAPTER 11

WHEN YOU'RE
BORED

Quick check-in

Ughh. How bored do I feel?

1 BEING QUITE BORED; 5 BEING "OMG, IF I ROLL MY EYES ANY MORE THEY'LL PERMANENTLY GET STUCK THAT WAY."

1   **2**   **3**   **4**   **5**

How uncomfortable do I feel?

1 BEING PRETTY UNCOMFORTABLE; 5 BEING "THIS IS BASICALLY PAINFUL."

What's going on when I typically feel bored?

I'M AT [LOCATION] . . .

....

....

....

DOING [ACTIVITY] . . .

....

....

....

AND I THINK IT'S BECAUSE [DEEPER REASON] . . .

....

....

....

CREATIVE YOU

PRETEND YOU'RE THESE THINGS, AND
DRAW WHAT YOU'D LOOK LIKE.

FLOWER

APP

OUTFIT

BOOK

MOVIE POSTER

FOOD

MUSICAL INSTRUMENT

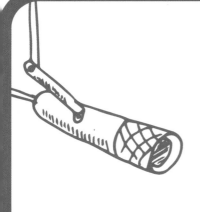

PRETEND YOU'RE A VLOGGER

WHAT'S YOUR CHANNEL ALL ABOUT?

LIST FIVE VIDEOS YOU'D CREATE FOR YOUR CHANNEL.

1
....
....

2
....
....

3
....
....

4
....
....

5
....
....

YOU'VE JUST ENTERED YOUR IMAGINATION

BECAUSE YOUR IMAGINATION IS SO WONDERFULLY VAST, IT'S REPRESENTED BY THESE THREE DOORS. WHAT SCENES, OBJECTS, AND SURPRISES DO YOU FIND INSIDE EACH DOOR?

DRAW, COLOR, OR PASTE DIFFERENT IMAGES AND FABRICS THAT REVEAL WHAT YOUR MAGICAL IMAGINATION LOOKS AND FEELS LIKE.

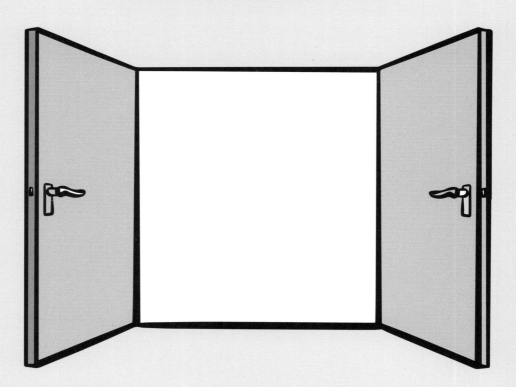

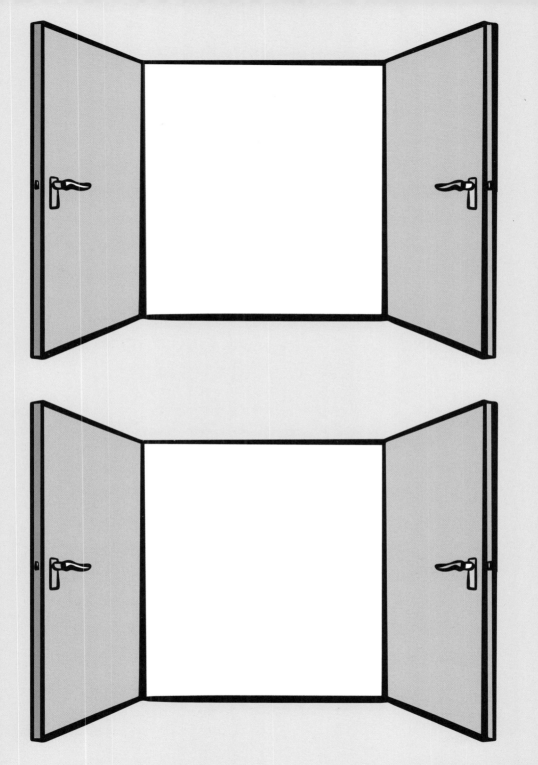

START A 30-DAY CREATIVE PROJECT

JOT DOWN WHAT YOU'LL DO ON EACH DAY FOR THE WHOLE MONTH, OR PUT YOUR CREATIVE PROJECT RIGHT ON YOUR CALENDAR—LIKE A TWO-LINE POEM, A NEW WORD YOU LEARN EVERY DAY, OR A QUICK DRAWING YOU DOODLE ON THE SCHOOL BUS.

MY **CREATIVE** MONTH

1	2	3
4	5	6
7	8	9

10	11	12
13	14	15
16	17	18
19	20	21
22	23	24
25	26	27
28	29	30

AN EXCITING DISCOVERY!

A TEAM OF SCIENTISTS HAS RECENTLY DISCOVERED
A NEW PLANET. DRAW IT HERE.

ADD A FEW DETAILS LIKE WHAT IT'S CALLED, WHO LIVES
THERE, AND WHAT THE RESIDENTS DO FOR FUN.

YOU FEEL LIKE YOU'RE THE ONLY ONE
WHO'S STRUGGLING IN MATH CLASS, FEELING INSECURE
AND UNCOMFORTABLE IN YOUR OWN SKIN, OR DEALING
WITH ANXIETY, DEPRESSION, OR ANOTHER MENTAL
HEALTH CONDITION. **BUT YOU'RE NOT.**

FOR INSTANCE, AROUND 17 MILLION KIDS AND TEENS
HAVE OR HAVE HAD A MENTAL ILLNESS. YOU'RE ALSO
NOT ALONE IN FEELING LONELY—DIFFERENT SURVEYS
SHOW THAT IT'S COMMON FOR KIDS AND TEENS
TO FEEL THIS WAY.

IN SHORT, **EVERYONE STRUGGLES** IN SOME WAY,
BECAUSE WE'RE HUMAN.

WHATEVER YOU'RE STRUGGLING WITH, **KNOW YOU'RE IN
GOOD COMPANY.** YOU REALLY ARE.

CHAPTER 12

WHEN YOU FEEL ALONE IN YOUR **STRUGGLES**

How alone do I feel right now?

1 BEING "IT'S HARD TO IMAGINE THAT ANYONE ELSE FEELS LIKE I DO";

5 BEING "NO ONE GETS IT. THEY NEVER WILL. AND IT'S JUST ME. ONLY ME."

How often do I feel alone?

☐ ALL THE TIME

☐ MOST OF THE TIME

☐ SOMETIMES

☐ THIS IS NEW FOR ME

RIGHT NOW, I'M FEELING TERRIBLY LONELY BECAUSE . . .

....

....

....

....

....

....

DRAW YOUR LONELINESS

WHAT DOES YOUR LONELINESS LOOK LIKE? WHAT DOES IT FEEL AND SOUND LIKE? WHAT DOES IT TASTE AND SMELL LIKE? GRAB SOME PENCILS AND DRAW IT ALL OUT HERE.

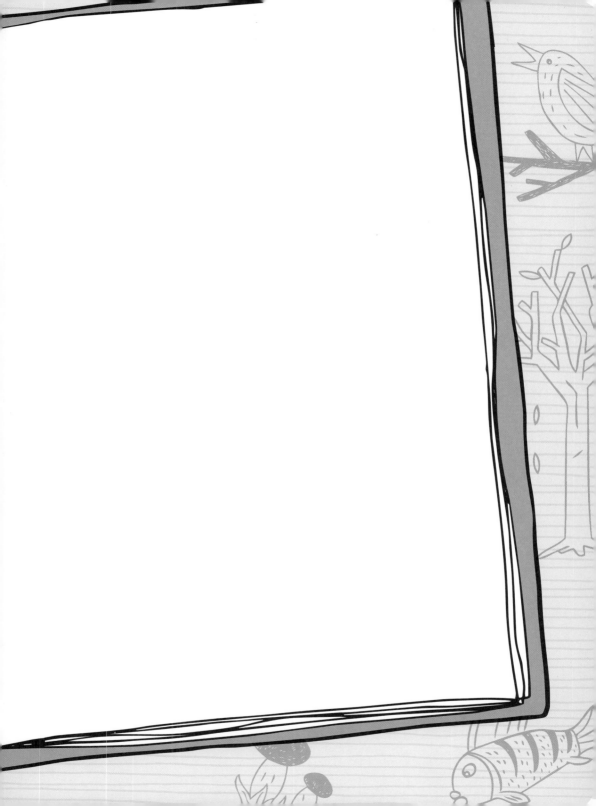

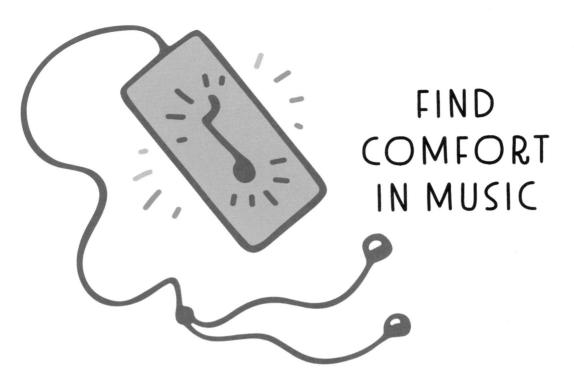

FIND COMFORT IN MUSIC

MAKE A LIST OF SONGS THAT HELP YOU FEEL
LESS ALONE, AND USE IT TO CREATE YOUR OWN
PLAYLIST ON YOUR PHONE.

....

....

....

....

....

....

....

NOW JOT DOWN THE LYRICS THAT ARE MOST
MEANINGFUL AND COMFORTING TO YOU.

WRITE A KIND, CARING LETTER . . .

. . . TO SOMEONE WHO'S STRUGGLING WITH
THE SAME THING YOU ARE.

Now read
this letter to
yourself.

STRUGGLING (AND HEALING) TOGETHER

GOOGLE WHATEVER YOU'RE STRUGGLING WITH—ANXIETY, DEPRESSION, DIABETES, FRIEND DRAMA—AND FIND SOMEONE WHO'S BEEN THERE, TOO.

READ THROUGH THEIR STORY—IN A PERSONAL ESSAY, BLOG, OR SOCIAL POST—AND FIND THE WORDS THAT COMFORT YOU AND REMIND YOU THAT YOU'RE NOT ALONE. WRITE THEM HERE.

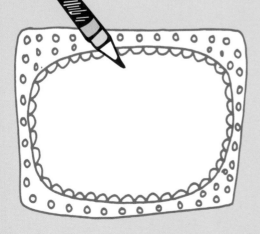

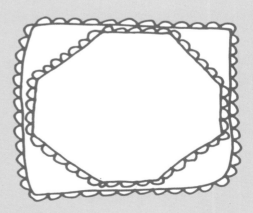

When you find
yourself struggling
again—because there are
natural ebbs and flows—
reread these words
and remember.

GETTING THE
SUPPORT
YOU NEED

TALKING TO SOMEONE WHO'S BEEN IN A SIMILAR SITUATION
CAN BE INCREDIBLY HELPFUL. BUT YOUR LOVED ONES DON'T
NEED TO EXPERIENCE THE SAME THINGS TO BE SUPPORTIVE.
TO HELP THEM HELP YOU, KINDLY AND CLEARLY SPELL OUT
THE TYPE OF SUPPORT YOU NEED RIGHT NOW.

Person:

Support I'd like:

....

....

....

....

....

....

Person: Support I'd like:

....

....

....

....

....

....

....

....

....

....

....

....

....

....

....

**SOME DAYS JUST FEEL HARD AND HEAVY,
AND YOU CAN'T SHAKE THE FEELING THAT
LIFE IS AWFUL AND BLEAK.**

BUT HERE'S A BRIGHT SPOT: YOU CAN LIGHTEN
THE DARKNESS BY RECOGNIZING YOUR NEGATIVE
THOUGHT LOOPS AND CHANGING THEM.
BECAUSE YOU DON'T HAVE TO BELIEVE
EVERYTHING YOU THINK.

THIS DOESN'T MEAN YOU SHOULD FAKE IT AND
PUT ON A HAPPY FACE (WHEN YOU'RE SOBBING
INSIDE). RATHER, WHEN EVERYTHING FEELS DARK
AND GLOOMY, YOU CAN EXPAND YOUR MINDSET,
FIND THE HUMOR, AND SEE THE NUANCE.
BECAUSE EVEN THE DARKNESS HAS SHADES OF GRAY.

CHAPTER 13
WHEN EVERYTHING FEELS
DARK AND GLOOMY

Quick check-in

How awful does the world look right now?

1 BEING PRETTY BAD; 5 BEING "WE'RE ALL DOOMED."

1   2   3   4   5

How often does everything seem dark and dreary?

- [ ] ALL THE TIME
- [ ] MOST OF THE TIME
- [ ] SOMETIMES
- [ ] THIS IS NEW FOR ME

Does a certain part of my life feel particularly bleak?

- [ ] YES
- [ ] NO

If yes, the darkness seems to be around:

- [ ] SCHOOL
- [ ] SPORTS
- [ ] A SPECIFIC CLASS
- [ ] MY PART-TIME JOB
- [ ] FRIENDS
- [ ] FAMILY
- [ ] CERTAIN PEOPLE
- [ ] SOMETHING ELSE

....

....

....

....

How often do I think "Why bother?" "No one cares," or "These dark clouds are here to stay"?

- [ ] ALL THE TIME
- [ ] MOST OF THE TIME
- [ ] SOMETIMES
- [ ] THIS IS NEW FOR ME

SHADES OF GRAY

TRAVEL INTO THE MURKY CORNERS OF YOUR MIND, WHERE THE NEGATIVE THOUGHTS RESIDE.

WHAT DO YOU FIND THERE?
WHY HAS THE LIGHT DIMMED?

NOW LET'S ADD SOME LIGHT TO YOUR DARK THOUGHTS
TO REVEAL SHADES OF GRAY.

WRITE THE THOUGHTS YOU'RE CURRENTLY THINKING.
CROSS OUT EXTREME WORDS AND ABSOLUTES,
AND REPLACE THEM WITH SOFTER, TRUER LANGUAGE, LIKE:

I ~~HATE~~ THIS PLACE! I don't like THIS PLACE.

I ~~CAN'T~~ FIGURE THIS OUT.

~~EVERYTHING~~ SUCKS!

 I'LL **try** TO FIGURE
THIS OUT, OR I
CAN'T FIGURE THIS
OUT **yet**.

Many PARTS OF MY LIFE FEEL
HARD RIGHT NOW, BUT OTHERS
FEEL FINE, EVEN GREAT.

DISASTER AWAITS!

LIFE CAN LOOK BLEAK WHEN YOUR MIND ASSUMES THE WORST, TURNING POTENTIALLY STRESSFUL OR SIGNIFICANT SITUATIONS INTO CATASTROPHES.

SO, GO WITH IT! DOUBLING DOWN ON DISASTROUS STORIES CAN ACTUALLY EASE ANXIETY, BECAUSE IT REMINDS US THAT SOMETIMES LIFE IS JUST SILLY—AND IT'S GOOD TO LOOK FOR THE HUMOR AND JUST LAUGH.

To start, pick a situation that your mind keeps telling you is going to implode, and invent an even more outlandish and absurd story of things going wrong.

Once upon a time . . .

....

....

....

....

....

....

....

....

....

....

....

....

....

....

....

....

....

Read your new story in your best pirate accent!

POSITIVE THOUGHTS, POSITIVE ACTIONS

NOW, THINK ABOUT THE POSITIVE RESULTS.

LIST ACTIONS YOU CAN TAKE THAT JUST MIGHT RESULT IN

A GOOD OUTCOME—OR SOMETHING PRETTY CLOSE.

....

....

....

....

....

....

....

In the margin, draw anything that makes you happy.

YOUR FEEL BETTER ACTION PLAN

From now on, when I feel . . .	. . . I'll take this healthy action:
From now on, when I feel . . .	. . . I'll take this healthy action:
From now on, when I feel . . .	. . . I'll take this healthy action:

When I need to vent, feel less alone, or ask for advice, I'll talk to:

....

When I need a good laugh, I'll watch, listen, or talk to:

....

....

When I'm struggling, I can say these kind words to myself:

....

....

When I need to relax, I can:

....

....

....

When I can't sleep, I will:

....

....

....

When I make a mistake, I'll remind myself:

....

....

....

When life feels hard or dark or scary, I will:

....

....

....

These are my favorite prompts, which I'll return to regularly:

Page	Page	Page	Page	Page

This week, I'm kicking off this creative project:

....

....

....

I'm always grateful for:

....

....

....

PLEASE REMEMBER,

IT'S NOT EASY TO FACE YOUR EMOTIONS AND CHANGE UNHELPFUL HABITS . . .

YOU'RE DOING IT,
...E DOING AN EXCELLENT JOB!

...dness and
...ade a mistake or
...of space. And on the
...ease treat yourself well,
an... ...ed to love or even like
yours... ...e self-compassion or choose
a healthi... ...t.

REMEMBER you are never alone in your struggles. Because, well, you're human.

REMEMBER that painful feelings are fleeting. An hour, day, week, month, or year from now, you will feel better. And you might even forget why you were so upset in the first place. Or, you'll grow from that difficult experience, becoming a stronger, more compassionate person, having a better idea of what you need, and knowing the people that are worthy of your love (and those that aren't).

REMEMBER, too, that you don't need to figure it all out on your own. When you feel lost or overwhelmed, reach out. Talk to someone who's already found their way out of the maze.

REMEMBER you are incredible, even if you can't see it.

FINDING HELP

For more on mental health visit:

The Jed Foundation: https://www.jedfoundation.org/
Active Minds: https://www.activeminds.org/
Our Minds Matter: https://ourmindsmatter.org/
This is My Brave: https://thisismybrave.org/

To talk to someone right away:

- Call 1-800-273-TALK (8255)
  at the National Suicide Prevention Lifeline:
  https://suicidepreventionlifeline.org/

- Text HOME to 741741 at the Crisis Text Line:
  https://www.crisistextline.org/text-us/

If you need a bit more support in feeling better, talk to your family about seeing a therapist. Remember that you are brave for working through your challenges. You might feel like the exact opposite. But the truth is:

It takes courage and strength to seek support.

AUTHOR ACKNOWLEDGMENTS

A heartfelt thank-you to:

Brian, Mama, Papa, and Babushka Lilya for loving me exactly as I am and making me feel like anything is possible. And for everything else. Papa and Babushka, I miss you every day.

Lily for being our world and making us laugh. May you always know how incredible you are.

Tetya Bella and Masha for your wisdom, humor, strength, and so much more.

Leva, Irena, and Sasha for always showing up.

My friends for being there and making my world brighter.

John Grohol, founder of PsychCentral.com, for the boundless kindness and creative freedom; for giving a newbie writer the opportunity of a lifetime.

My current and past editors for being generous teachers.

The Quarto team for choosing me to write this book, making my words come alive, and being wonderful to work with.